# SECRETS OF THE MIND

# SECRETS
*of*
*the* # MIND

## RALPH WALDO EMERSON'S KEYS
## TO EXPANSIVE MENTAL POWERS

# SAM TORODE

*That river flowing from whence I do not see,*
*Pours for a season its streams into me.*

RALPH WALDO EMERSON

# CONTENTS

# Foreword

*The mind is the supreme fact we know.*
*It is the commander of matter.*
*It is the life and order by which matter exists.*

RALPH WALDO EMERSON

EARLY in his career as a lecturer and essayist, Ralph Waldo Emerson set a goal to write "the natural history of the intellect." This, he believed, was his life's work—his highest aspiration and greatest challenge.

By "natural history," he meant science. Natural history is the study of organisms and objects in their environment, relying on close, first-hand observation. And by "intellect," he meant the mind. Thus, Emerson's aim was to explore and elucidate *the science of mind.*

It was, he often lamented, an impossible task—for the mind cannot be observed by the senses or examined by scientific instruments. Everything we perceive comes through the mind, but we cannot perceive the mind itself. Emerson could only observe its fruits, and from them try to deduce what this source called "mind" is like.

He began by rigorously observing the workings of his own mind. Beginning in college, he kept detailed journals of his thoughts, ideas, and memories. In mature years, he went so far as to index these voluminous journals by topic. They were his personal mine, in which he searched for rough gems to polish into lectures, essays, and poems.

He also studied the workings of the mind in history and nature. History, to Emerson, was the record of humanity's ideas through time. And everything in nature, he believed, had a corollary in the realm of thought.

From his home in Concord, Massachusetts, and on his travels around the United States and to Europe and England, Emerson searched for "the spirit of the times." New inventions, industries, emerging trends in politics, religion, and social mores—to Emerson, each was a manifestation of the mind in action.

Whatever he studied, wherever he went, Emerson looked past surface appearances to find their mental motivations, their root causes in the mind.

*E*MERSON'S continued efforts to catalog and chronicle the workings of the mind helped establish the new field of psychology. William James (1842–1910), who is often called the first American psychologist, was in fact Emerson's godson and was deeply influenced by him.

The Greek word *psyche* refers to the soul—our essence. True psychologists are those who, like Emerson and James, help us recover a sense of meaning and purpose when we feel disconnected from our deepest selves. In the Twentieth Century, Carl Jung stood out as an exemplar of this; as did Viktor Frankl, Holocaust survivor and author of *Man's Search for Meaning*.

Unfortunately, most psychologists, following Sigmund Freud, focused their attention on mental illness and disorder rather than health. But in the 1990s, a new school emerged—Positive Psychology. Its founders, Martin Seligman and Mihaly Csikszentmihalyi, described it as "a science of positive subjective experience, positive individual traits, and positive institutions, which promises to improve quality of life and prevent the pathologies that arise when life is barren and meaningless."

Emerson, no doubt, would be pleased by this furthering of the work he began.

*E*MERSON described his philosophy, Transcenden-talism, as an updated version of Plato's Idealism. Both stress the primacy of mind, in opposition to mate-rialism—the belief that matter is all that exists.

In Emerson's time, materialism was gaining traction among intellectuals. An influential model of the mind was John Locke's *tabula rasa*, which asserted that each person's mind, at birth, is a "blank slate" upon which the data provided by our senses is recorded as we inter-act with the physical world. All of the contents of the mind, according to this theory, come from sensory experience.

Emerson, by contrast, argued that we are each born with access to a transcendent, universal mind, which is the source of all thought and ideas. There are concepts we grasp intuitively, and ideas that grab us in moments of inspiration, which come from beyond our sensory experiences. The realm of thought *transcends* our indi-vidual bodies and brains—hence, the name Transcen-dentalism.

In the late 1800s and throughout the Twentieth Cen-tury, materialism became entrenched as the dominant philosophy among scientists and academics. Today, it's widely held that our minds are merely byproducts of the electro-chemical activity in our brains. Our thoughts are the result of neurons (brain cells) firing and forming connections. And because mental activity is limited to our individual brains, our minds are completely separate from each other.

Francis Crick, co-discoverer of the structure of DNA, summed it up this way:

> "You," your joys and your sorrows, your memories and ambitions, your sense of personal identity and free will, are in fact no more than the behavior of a vast assembly of nerve cells and their assorted molecules. . . . You are nothing but a pack of neurons.

If our minds are reducible to the random, purposeless, unconscious activity of brain cells, then our intuitive, instinctual senses of self, meaning, purpose, and free will—the very things that define our humanity—are all illusory. Some even assert that consciousness—our very awareness of being—is an illusion.

Why are Crick and other materialists so confident in the truth of their ideas? Materialism gives them no reason to suppose that human thoughts have any relation to reality at all.

*T*HOUGH Emerson lived long before modern brain science, I believe that Transcendentalism offers a far more compelling view of the mind than materialism.

In the Transcendentalist view, our brains allow us to access certain frequencies of mind; they don't create the mind. The firing of neurons is *correlated* with thought, but does not *cause* thought.*

The brain, then, is like a radio receiver that picks up invisible waves broadcast from beyond itself. Or, to use another analogy, the brain is like a computer, which can do nothing without being programmed and operated by an intelligence beyond its wires and circuits.

This is not to devalue the brain—it's a priceless piece of hardware, and we should care for it accordingly. For also like a computer, our brain is vulnerable to damage and aging, which make it less capable of receiving, processing, and expressing thoughts.

As technology has advanced exponentially over the past few decades, so the human brain has made astound-

---

* Recent experiments have shown that by choosing and repeating new thoughts, we can create new neural pathways and actually change the physical structure of the brain. Neuroplasticity is a powerful affirmation of free will and the primacy of mind over matter.

ing leaps in complexity and capacity over the past few hundred thousand years.

But here's where the radio and computer analogies break down: The brain is not an unchanging mechanism designed, built, and programmed by an outside engineer. It's an organic part of the living, evolving, self-organizing, intelligent, conscious universe to which we belong.

$I$N his important book *Science Set Free* (2012), biologist Rupert Sheldrake challenges the materialist view of mind and nature. He presents compelling scientific evidence that the mind is not limited to the brain; that memories aren't stored in neurons; that our choices are not predetermined by our biochemistry; and that psychic phenomena such as telepathy sometimes really occur.

Another essential book in this vein is *One Mind* (2013) by Larry Dossey. As a teenager, Dossey stumbled across a volume of Emerson's essays in a soda shop, which introduced him to the concept that we all share one mind. But he remained skeptical until his experiences and research as a medical doctor confirmed it.

The arguments made by Sheldrake, Dossey, and others (including Bruce Lipton, Dean Radin, Bernardo

Kastrup, Deepak Chopra, Eben Alexander, and Lynne McTaggart) haven't been disproven by science—quite the opposite—but they've been rejected out of hand by materialist dogma. The history of science is replete with examples of new theories that were laughed at, ignored, attacked, and—at long last—accepted. When it comes to the transcendency of mind over matter, another such paradigm shift may be underway.

This debate—materialism versus Transcendentalism—isn't just academic. It's of interest to each and every one of us, for philosophies have consequences. Someone who believes that their mind is a byproduct of their brain, and that all their thoughts, choices, and actions are determined by purposeless forces in a meaningless universe, is liable to think, feel, and act differently than someone who believes that they're connected to all others through the universal mind, that they're responsible for their own thoughts, choices, and actions, and that their life has meaning and purpose. (Unless, of course, a person's way of living is in conflict with their intellectually-held beliefs, which is often the case. Many self-professed materialists are kind, generous champions for the common good, while some spiritual believers harm others in their pursuit of material pleasure and comfort.)

$\mathcal{E}$MERSON'S philosophy has the power to change the way you view the world and your place in it. It might even change your life.

*Secrets of the Mind* paraphrases and brings together Emerson's most important essays and lectures on the subject of mind. It's a companion to my previous book, *Living from the Soul*, which distills his spiritual teachings.

Mind and soul are words describing the great intangible Source expressing itself through what we experience as physical reality. It's impossible to separate the two, except perhaps to say that the soul encompasses all, including the mind.

On the individual level, our souls are greater than our minds. On the universal level, soul and mind are both infinite. This is why Emerson used the terms "universal mind" and "universal soul" (or "oversoul") interchangeably.

As individuals, we can roughly distinguish between the mental and spiritual aspects of our lives. *Living from the Soul* focuses on the spiritual, while *Secrets of the Mind* focuses on the mental. Appropriately, this book is more complex and cerebral than its predecessor; but if you've read this far, you'll have no trouble understanding it.

Emerson's method was circular—he returned to the same ideas again and again, using different words and examples. Most of his lectures and essays are variations on one theme: that we are all expressions of the universal mind or soul. Within that great theme, various sub-themes recur. This helps us better grasp and retain them, which is why I've chosen not to eliminate all repetition from this book. As with *Living from the Soul*, I've also interspersed resonant quotes from other authors that echo and expand upon Emerson's insights.

My motivation in creating these paraphrase editions is personal. I can't think of a better way to start the day than reading my favorite author, pondering his thoughts, wrestling with difficult passages, and rephrasing them in my own way. It's joyful, satisfying work.

Emerson challenges us to think better, and to think about better things. By reading and meditating upon his ideas, we succeed at both. My hope is that this presentation of his philosophy will inspire you to open your mind, introduce you to new powers and possibilities, and enrich your days.

—SAM TORODE

# CHAPTER I

# The Universal Mind

# 1

THERE is one mind common to all humanity. The universal mind is a vast ocean, of which your mind—and everyone else's—is an inlet.

Through the mind, you are connected to all that has been done, is being done, and can be done. The thoughts Socrates thought, you can think; the way St. Francis felt, you can feel; the fears and struggles others have faced, you can face and empathize with.

We see the same human mind at work in all times, places, and races. As the Roman playwright Terrance said, "I am human, and nothing human is foreign to me."

The ancestor of every act is a thought. Every revolution begins as an idea in one person's mind. As the same thought occurs in others, or is heard and accepted by them, it builds momentum. If an idea—like democracy, liberty, or civil rights—gains enough power, it can define an entire era.

History is the record of the human mind over time. Egypt, Greece, Rome, India, China, America—every civilization and culture is the work of the mind, as expressed through particular people in their place and time.

The same mind that wrote history reads it. The past is never past. When you are excited by the same idea that excited Plato; when you are awed by the same principle that awed Newton; when you are moved by the same beauty that moved Sappho, time ceases to exist.

This one mind is our priceless inheritance. It's up to you to take possession of it, explore its boundless reaches, and exercise its powers wisely for the benefit of all.

*A felt unity with all other minds conveys*
*renewed meaning, purpose, and possibility*
*and a sense of the sacredness of all things.*
**LARRY DOSSEY**
medical doctor and philosopher

## INVISIBLE, INTANGIBLE, INEFFABLE

No science would be of greater value than a science of the mind. If only we could map the mind's contours, mark its boundaries, describe its habits, and write its natural history. But who can examine an invisible essence?

The mind defies dissection. We can describe its various powers, but we can't separate them. Perception, reason, imagination, instinct, memory, calculation, will—each blends into the other.

The mind is not a sense organ, like the eye that sees or the ear that hears. For the mind not only thinks and knows, but is *one with* all that is thought and known. And so it remains ever elusive, ever mysterious.

*What is mind? The mind is the medium*
*of everything you have ever known, seen, or felt;*
*everything that has ever meant anything*
*to you. It is that which perceives.*
**BERNARDO KASTRUP**
computer scientist and philosopher

## Beyond Sensations & Emotions

Sensory data and emotions form a portion of our mental landscape, but the mind extends far beyond them.

Some people trust only in their physical senses. If something can't be seen, heard, touched, tasted, or smelled, it doesn't exist. They distrust intuition, imagination, and abstract ideas. But all of the information provided by our senses would be a senseless jumble without the mind's abstract, interpretive powers.

To our senses, each thing appears separate and distinct. It's the intuitive, abstractive mind that pierces surfaces, leaps walls, makes connections, organizes, conceptualizes, and distills a multitude of phenomena into a few principles. Our experience of the tangible world depends entirely on our intangible mind.

Others trust mainly in their emotions. What they think about something depends on how they *feel* about it. They distrust reason and logic. But since feelings often change, it's impossible for them to walk in a straight line without being tugged this way or that.

Heraclitus likened our emotional states to colored mists hovering before our eyes, changing hue from one hour to the next. Reason lifts the veil and shows us what *is*, apart from our personal likes, dislikes, and fears.

In your mind's eye, you have the ability to see your-self and your circumstances from a distance, as if you were observing someone else. The goal is not to elimi-nate your emotions, which are a rich and vital aspect of life, but to avoid being blinded and controlled by them.

> *Our minds can embrace possibilities that go far beyond our own experience. Conscious minds choose among possibilities, and their choices collapse possibilities into actions that are objectively observable in the physical world.*
>
> RUPERT SHELDRAKE
> biologist and philosopher

## TRANSMUTING LIFE INTO THOUGHT

Everyone views the human condition with some degree of melancholy. Like a ship tossed by the waves, we are at the mercy of oncoming events. But once a storm has passed, it is taken up by the mind as fuel for thought and no longer threatens us. Any fact of our life can be made an object for reflection; and when facts are transmuted into lessons and truths, we behold them as immortal gods.

You can't force the mind or rush its process. You can only open yourself up, clear away any obstructions or distractions, and let the mind see what it sees. The more spontaneous your thoughts, the better.

We don't get ideas so much as they get us. They swoop down, carry us up to their ethereal realm, and engage our attention such that we can think of nothing else. By and by, when we fall out of that rapture, we try our best to remember them and repeat them to others.

Thoughts germinate, grow, and blossom like plants. First you have an intuition, then an opinion, and then—if it thrives in the light of observation and experience—knowledge. Cherish your intuitions, for one day they may ripen into truths.

Each mind has its own method, as well as its own storehouse of accumulated facts upon which to draw. Differences in intellectual endowment are insignificant compared with our common wealth. Do you think that the cashier, the cook, and the trash collector have no thoughts, no stories, no wonders for you? Be curious about the ways others live and think, including—or especially—those with little formal schooling. Your curiosity will be rewarded.

> *All sorrows can be borne if you put them*
> *into a story or tell a story about them.*
> **KAREN BLIXEN**
> Dutch writer, pen name Isak Dinesen

## THE STOREHOUSE OF THOUGHT

The hardest task in the world is to think—to ponder important questions and remain open to new ideas, as we go about our day's activities. Most of the time, our thoughts flitter from one trifle to another. If only we could enter our mind and find it as quiet and orderly as a library!

It seems that mental activity must ebb and flow, inhale and exhale. As you read, converse, and act in the world, your mind takes in vast amounts of raw material; then—at unpredictable intervals—it sends out polished thoughts. One minute, your mind seems like a dark attic full of rubbish; then inspiration lights the lamp of truth, and all your accumulated facts appear as treasures.

You may hear a delightful line from Shakespeare and ask, "How did he come up with that?"—as if he were more than human. But you have a storehouse of material just as good as Shakespeare's; you only need the lamp to illumine it and the skill to put it to good use.

If you could meet Shakespeare, you'd be struck more by your shared humanity than any difference. You might think, "Here's a person with unusual abilities of expression," but you wouldn't feel inferior in his presence. If anything, his wit and eloquence would serve to bring out your own.

*There is nothing either good or bad,*
*but thinking makes it so.*
**WILLIAM SHAKESPEARE**
English playwright

*I have thrown my life into the work—*
*my single, simple life; pouring it into the book;*
*honestly, without stint, giving the book all, all, all.*
**WALT WHITMAN**
American poet

## FINDING YOUR GENIUS

We are all wise, and each have our own unique genius. How can you find yours? By taking the facts and circumstances of your life and, through the power of your mind, using them constructively—to build, to create, to uplift others.

Genius is intellect in action. It requires inspiration *and* expression.

If an idea enters your mind but you never put it into words, act on it, or give it form, it's of no consequence. The most wonderful inspirations will die with you if you don't have the skill, desire, or determination to express them.

Inspiration is spontaneous, but expression requires control, willpower, judgment, and choice—otherwise nothing can be produced.

Great art doesn't flow only—or even primarily—from one's experiences, or from imitating the work of others; the fountainhead is much deeper and richer.

Dreams offer a clue. You may not be able to draw a human figure to save your life; yet when you're asleep, what a marvelous artist you are! In the dream state, you fill the canvas with people, creatures, and a myriad of forms lifelike enough to spark wonder, desire, sadness, and terror.

If you can create such a world in your dreams, the source of all art and invention must lie within your mind. You only need the skill and will to manifest its bounty.

*Your purpose is to become conscious of your genius that is one with all, and express your genius by bringing your special contribution to life.*

TIM FREKE
English philosopher

## MAINTAINING BALANCE

Air and water are essential; but if a person takes in too much of either, they'll become sick and may even die. Thoughts are essential, too. But if a person latches onto *one* thought to the neglect of others, even truth becomes distorted into falsehood.

An idea can be a portal or a prison. How wearisome

are the religious fanatics, political ideologues, and intellectual zealots who think their one idea explains everything!

How can we avoid mental myopia? By attempting to study all of science and history, memorizing every name, date, and fact? No—the world refuses to be reduced to facts.

A healthy mind is a whole mind, mirroring the wholeness of nature. The universe is vast beyond comprehension, but nature repeats itself in miniature in all its works. All of the laws of nature are found in every part of nature.

So, while we cannot hope to carry all things in our individual minds, we can humbly strive to reflect the balance and proportion of the universal mind, which holds all.

*Until you realize that many things you were*
*sure of are not so, and many you scoffed at*
*are true, you have not yet begun to live.*
**ELBERT HUBBARD**
founder, Roycroft Arts & Crafts community

## THE SCHOOL OF SOVEREIGN MINDS

Over the course of our life, we progress through a series of teachers. For a time, we sit at the feet of one master; then we move on to another.

Accept all your teachers, past and present, as part of your development. Listen to them, wrestle with them, take all they have to give with thanks, and then leave. May they become like serene stars shining in your sky, blending their lights with your own sun—instead of blocking it out.

There are two mischievous superstitions that do us harm. One is "I am wiser than you," and the other is "You are wiser than me." The truth is, each of us is equipped with the wisdom we need to steer our own boat, if we only listen to the voice of our inner pilot instead of mimicking our neighbors' motions.

While belonging to the universal mind, each person must rely on their own portion. Respect others as sovereign minds, and respect yourself as a sovereign mind. Homer's *Odyssey* may have delighted Europe for over a thousand years; but what good is that if it doesn't delight *you*?

Approach philosophy the same way. Anyone who proposes a theory of the mind—be it Descartes, Kant,

Spinoza, Hume, Hegel, or anyone else—is only a more or less accurate translator of things in your own consciousness, to which you have direct access.

With any teacher or book, take what resonates with you and leave the rest. Your own mind is your greatest teacher. Trust it.

*What you think of yourself,*
*that is what determines your fate.*
**HENRY DAVID THOREAU**
ecologist and Transcendentalist philosopher

## KEY IDEAS

1. There is one mind common to all humanity.

2. The ancestor of every act is a thought.

3. History is the record of the human mind over time.

4. We don't get ideas so much as they get us.

5. Cherish your intuitions, for one day they may ripen into truths.

6. We are all wise, and each have our own unique genius.

7. Genius is intellect in action.

8. An idea can be a portal or a prison.

9. A healthy mind is a whole mind, mirroring the wholeness of nature.

10. Your own mind is your greatest teacher.

# Principles & Powers of Thought

# 2

WE delight in hearing scientists explain the workings of the human body, the secret lives of plants, the origins of rocks and mountains, the principles of electricity and magnetism, and all the wonders of nature. So serene and sure are they in their facts! The broadest of their facts—the ones that cover a multitude of phenomena—they even called "laws."

Could a similar survey be made of the mind, describing its workings and laws? After all, our thoughts are part of nature—though of a high order, near to the mysterious source of creation.

The unique challenge in examining the mind from a scientific standpoint is that the mind is both the observer and the observed. Intellectual distance and objectivity are impossible when you *think* about *thought*.

That said, nothing is more worthy of rigorous study than the mind, and no scientific contribution would be more valuable than elucidating the principles and powers of thought.

> *The substrate of mind cannot be measured,*
> *detected, or analyzed like some kind of stuff,*
> *because it is that which measures, detects, and*
> *analyzes in the first place. Mind is not a material,*
> *but that which imagines all materials.*
> **BERNARDO KASTRUP**

## LANGUAGES & LAWS

When we study any part of nature, and finally grasp the principle behind it, we gain a new power. Best of all is when a principle relating to one phenomenon shines new light on many other phenomena in different fields of inquiry—this is the discovery of a law.

All the languages of the world are but dialects of one universal speech. The symbols and sounds used by each tribe differ, but the meanings to which they refer are the same.

Similarly, each field of human endeavor has its own set of facts and principles, which have analogues in every other field. For instance, Johannes Kepler showed that the laws of astronomy echo the laws of music, and the principles and proportions of one can be deduced from the other.

The laws of thought ultimately will be found to parallel the laws of astronomy, anatomy, algebra, and every other field of study. Every physical truth is symbolic of a mental truth; for everything in the physical world is an expression of mind. (This will be explored in detail in the next chapter.)

*There is one universe comprising all things;*
*one divine power from which the universe arose*
*and by which it is sustained; one set of laws*
*governing all natural phenomena; one life*
*shared by all living beings; and one reason*
*shared by all thinking people.*
MARCUS AURELIUS
Roman emperor and philosopher

## THE VALUE OF FINE THOUGHTS

No aspect of our life is more essential than the mental. What else elevates humanity above mere animal existence? Each step into deeper thought ennobles us. Moreover, there's a thrill of pleasure that comes with each new insight and idea. Our minds crave good thoughts as our bodies crave good food. In fact, most of us can think of times we were so absorbed in thought that we forgot to eat.

The story is told that Phaedrus held up a rare philosophical manuscript before Socrates and quipped that, by keeping it just out of reach, he could lead Socrates to the ends of the earth as one leads a mule with a handful of hay. Such is the lure of fine thoughts!

The most prized things in life are not physical, but mental and spiritual. What garners the most applause in the theater? Depictions of love and courage. What unites a crowd and melts away political differences? Words of justice, freedom, and generosity. Which books have been the most widely published and read and over the centuries? Works of mythology, theology, and philosophy, dealing with mind and soul. These subjects have enduring appeal to people of all races, classes, and walks of life.

*Nothing delights the mind as much as virtue—especially when we see it embodied in the life of a particular person. This is why stories of bravery, self-sacrifice, and heroism never grow old.*
**MARCUS AURELIUS**

## The Creative Power of Thought

Where did all of humanity's tools, inventions, governments, religions, arts, and sciences come from? Out of the universal mind, of which we all partake.

Certain trees draw nearly all of their sustenance from the air. Plant a pine in a sandbank where there is no fertile soil, and still it will thrive on sunlight and moisture. Similarly, the arts and institutions of humanity are created out of invisible thought.

Intellect, inspiration, and willpower give rise to cities and civilizations. Lasting systems of government are based on shared ideals, not brute force. Even industry, banking, and trade rest on mental foundations.

Every truth becomes a power. Every idea, from the moment of its conception, begins to gather material forces, and soon makes itself known in the spheres of commerce and politics. Ideas clothe themselves in gowns, coats, and shoes, and shelter themselves in houses, temples, and halls of government. Thoughts become things.

As rain falls first on the mountain and then runs down into the valley, ideas fall first on elevated minds, then run down to the rest of humanity. On the banks of a river that flows from the mountain, a city will arise.

*Mind is the master power that molds and makes;*
*We are mind, in one of the guises it takes.*
*Taking the tool of thought, we sculpt what we will,*
*Shaping our lives for good or ill.*
*We think in secret, and it comes to pass;*
*The world is our reflection—the mind's looking-glass.*

**JAMES ALLEN**
English philosopher

## BALANCING ACTION & CONTEMPLATION

Some view life primarily as an arena for action. They find fulfillment in expressing their talents and abilities in practical ways, for the enjoyment of themselves and others. Others view life primarily as a school for mental and spiritual elevation. They can sit for hours in rapt contemplation of an idea.

Society is always a balance of these two types—the active and the contemplative. Even within each individual, both tendencies exist.

Today, we are out of balance. Never before has the call for action, practicality, and results so drowned out the quiet voice of contemplation. Even in our universities, Plato's works are analyzed as ancient Greek texts, rather than meditated upon as sources of insight and truth.

The highest service you can render to humanity is not to build a new machine for transportation or device for communication, as helpful as that might be, but to bring us a ray of divine light.

*Knowledge and love are revealed as the two cosmic forces which are apparently separate in nature but which spring from the same power and source.*
GIORDANO BRUNO
Italian scientist, monk, and martyr

## As You Think, So You Are

Looking within ourselves, we can distinguish at least three powers of perception: insight, memory, and imagination. We should exercise and improve our capacity for each, to the best of our ability. Even a small increase in mental power translates into a vast increase in outward power.

Though invisible and intangible, knowledge outweighs physical adversity. The guide who knows the way can scale the mountain in the dark. The sailor who knows the rigging and working of her boat can face seas that would drown another.

Knowledge is true power. Those who *know* are calm and secure, with no need to put on a show to hide their ignorance.

A large part of wisdom is being open to new knowledge and resisting the tendency to rigidity of thought. What we need is not greater speed in acting, but greater patience and reverence before the source of action—the mind.

What is your life, but what you think about all day? This is your occupation and your fate. "You are what you know," the Latin proverb says.

As one whose eye catches the glint of a crystal amidst the gray rocks, so occasionally we catch the glimmer of a truth amidst our dull, daily thoughts. We take that gem home and add it to our collection, which grows year after year.

*Diamonds are obtained by mining under the earth.*
*Dig deep within your soul, and you'll gain new*
*riches of understanding, wisdom, and power.*
**JAMES ALLEN**

## The Healing Power
## of Meditation

Blessed is the realm of thought; serene pleasures there abide. There's medicinal value in soaking in its healing springs. Excessive physical labor starves us in one way; excessive pampering in another. But a retreat into the mind restores and refreshes us. Great and noble thoughts are of universal and enduring value.

When we connect with mind and spirit, we cannot help but feel the mental and spiritual nature of the universe. In the hour of meditation, the senses take leave and physical things lose their importance. The struggles and sorrows of this world are transmuted into principles and truths, which we behold without pain.

Contrary to all pronouncements of doubt and despair, the best is yet to come. The highest goods are within our reach. Not everyone can acquire a great deal of money, but money is only symbolic of human values. Music and poetry are other, better representations of the riches available to us all. "The true coin for which all else ought to be exchangeable," Plato wrote, "is a right understanding of that which is good."

*People long to escape life's struggles and*
*relax in country houses, by the seaside, or*
*in the mountains. But it is within your power to*
*find solace at any time, by retreating into yourself.*
*When your thoughts are orderly and tranquil,*
*there's no place quieter and more peaceful*
*than your own soul. There, you are free.*
MARCUS AURELIUS

## The Teaching Power of Memory

Have you ever sailed in a boat and watched the wake trailing behind? The fanning waves are a beautiful sight. Memory is the wake of the mind. The further we journey forward in life, the longer our wake stretches behind, and the more beautiful and useful it becomes.

Where are all your past thoughts now? Look at the wake behind you. If your wake is short and shallow, the reason is that your thoughts have been shallow. The deeper the thought, the more powerful the waves it creates.

It's a law of nature that you can only keep what you use. The fish that swim in the pitch-black waters of Mammoth Cave are blind; when sight is useless, nature does away with it. Such is the eternal relation between power and use. If you want to keep your memory sharp, exercise it.

The key to strengthening your memory is to strengthen your affections. If something leaves a strong impression on your emotions, you won't soon forget it. We best remember those things we love or hate.

Memory isn't made rich by the accumulation of superfluous odds and ends, but by the stockpiling of essentials. Be careful what thoughts and feelings you store in your memory. It eagerly clings to insults and injuries, empty words, superstitions, and old routines. Forget what ought to be forgotten.

There is both conscious and unconscious memory. Our conscious memory is slight compared to the unconscious, which holds everything we've ever experienced. Sometimes in dreams, we remember people and places from long ago, down to the finest detail—things we could never recall during waking hours.

Memory is not dead. It's a living companion, teacher, and guardian angel. Have you committed acts of selfishness, anger, and carelessness that are painful to remember? That's as it should be. Your memory will torment you until you are incapable of doing such things again; and when that day comes, you'll be set free.

By holding together past and present, memory gives continuity and dignity to our life. It's our own personal scripture, written day by day from birth onward, which records all that we perceive, distills its meaning, and explains the world back to us.

*How does memory work? Most people take it for granted that memories must be stored in the brain as material traces, yet attempts to locate memory stores have proven unsuccessful over and over again. The alternative is the resonance theory: memories are transferred by resonance*

*from similar patterns of activity in the past.
We tune into ourselves from the past; we do not
carry our memories around inside our heads.*

**RUPERT SHELDRAKE**

## CONSCIOUS & UNCONSCIOUS THOUGHT

Nature endowed us with brains to facilitate the transmission and expression of thoughts; and so, our thoughts are inseparable from nature. The philosopher is as much a child of nature as the farmer, and the poet as the warrior.

Thoughts are part of the mind, but the mind is not limited to thoughts. The soul of a person, the soul of a plant—that which makes each part of nature what it is—these are all expressions of mind. Like fragments of ice floating in the arctic sea, so are our individual egos with their personal thoughts within the universal mind from which they emerged.

Our conscious thoughts represent only a tiny fraction of the mind's power. The thoughts that form our bodies, maintain our organs, and mold our personalities are unconscious and involuntary.

Each person is mind embodied. The history of the world is nothing but the procession of thoughts made flesh, ideas incarnate.

*The vision that you hold in your mind, the ideal*
*that you cherish in your heart—this you will build*
*your life by, and this you will become.*
JAMES ALLEN

## Your Potential for Greatness

All humanity thrills at the performance of a genius—
a Michelangelo, a Shakespeare, or a Mozart. This is a
sign that we each possess hidden gifts waiting to be
expressed. Don't look to the average person and assume
that most of us are born to be mediocre; look to the
best and aspire to be like them. You are no less human
than they. Through the universal mind, you have access to powers far greater than those you already know.

Our doctors tend to focus on pathology—diseases
and disorders of the mind. Little attention is paid to
those who are healthy, happy, and high-achieving. This
leads many to doubt their own potential.

Health of mind goes with health of body. When
your senses and faculties are sharp, you're capable of
insights far beyond what's possible in a state of dull-
ness or stupor.

When your senses are clear and your mind is open,
you'll find that the whole world shines with divine light.
The harvest is always bountiful, and the oracle is never

silent. All that's necessary is to be prepared to receive its messages faithfully and send them out again.

The mark of wisdom and goodness, in every field of human endeavor, is that they fill us with freedom and delight. Fear and hatred are signs that you're off the proper path. For at the center of the universe is a Heart, and with each beat it sends a flood of happiness into every artery and vein, so that the whole system is infused with joy.

*When your eyes become attuned to Nature
and her works, everything is beautiful.*
**MARCUS AURELIUS**

*The eye is the lamp of the body. If your eye is
clear, your whole body will be full of light.*
**JESUS OF NAZARETH**

## KEY IDEAS

1.  Every physical truth is symbolic of a mental truth.

2.  Our minds crave good thoughts as our bodies crave good food.

3.  The most prized things in life are not physical, but mental and spiritual.

4.  Thoughts become things.

5.  What is your life, but what you think about all day?

6.  A retreat into the mind restores and refreshes us.

7.  To strengthen your memory, strengthen your affections.

8.  Each person is mind embodied.

9.  We each possess hidden gifts waiting to be expressed.

10. The mark of wisdom and goodness is that they fill us with freedom and delight.

# CHAPTER 3

# Nature:
# The Mind's Mirror

# 3

*To see a World in a Grain of Sand*
*And a Heaven in a Wild Flower*
*Hold Infinity in the palm of your hand*
*And Eternity in an hour.*

**WILLIAM BLAKE**
English poet

PONDERING the principles and powers of thought, we're struck by the delightful correspondence between nature and mind. Natural objects and processes are symbolic of mental concepts and processes, and vice versa. The world around us and the world within us mirror each other. Both appear to spring from one source.

Wherever we look in nature—at flowers, fungi, atoms, oceans, or stars—our own reflection comes staring back at us. Pick up a scientific book on on any subject and you'll find it full of truths that, by analogy, apply to your own life.

Every science seems to be the study of humanity in disguise. From the facts and laws of any area of study, the workings of the mind can be inferred. A biologist could explain her thought processes using analogies drawn from biology; a chemist from chemistry; a physicist from physics; and so on.

This is serendipitous, because the mind can't be observed directly—only described by analogy.

*What you are in your inmost being escapes*
*your examination in rather the same way that you*
*cannot look directly into your own eyes without*
*using a mirror, you can't bite your own teeth,*
*and you can't taste your own tongue.*

**ALAN WATTS**
Zen philosopher

## PLANTS & PEOPLE

Botany—the study of plants—is especially rich with illustrations of mental phenomena. From infancy to old age, the growth of our mind mirrors the life cycle of a plant. What happens in our fields and gardens happens within us, too.

Curious resemblances to plants pervade humanity—our bodies as well as our minds. Both physically and mentally, we share the experiences of germination, growth, and reproduction, and we're subject to blights, parasites, and wilting. Anything that benefits or befalls a plant can benefit or befall us.

Plants and people are products of nature's ever evolving, self-organizing power. Our bodies and minds continue to develop whether we're awake or asleep, active or stagnant. We're always growing and learning, by day and by night.

Knowledge begins as a seed, which sprouts, buds, and flowers in our mind, then bears fruit in action. And under every leaf of thought is the bud of another waiting to emerge.

Some plants begin to bud in spring, but when the summer heat arrives they dry up and wilt. The same thing happens in people when a new thought is choked off and never comes to fruition.

Just as plants need nutrients from the soil and air to grow and reproduce, our minds thrive on nourishing food for thought. The more we fertilize our minds with new facts and experiences, the more fruit they bear.

*Resolve to know the laws of nature.*
*Follow them in all circumstances; let them shape*
*you; be guided by their perfect wisdom.*

EPICTETUS
Greek philosopher

## GROWING BETTER THOUGHTS

Jean-Baptiste Van Mons, who created many new varieties of pears through selective breeding, said, "I have found this art to consist in regenerating in a direct line of descent, as rapidly as possible. My secret is to sow, and sow, and resow—in short to do nothing but sow."

Conventional minds cling to one thought and don't go beyond it. Creative minds are characterized by taking one good thought and adding a second to it, then a third, and so on, multiplying the power of the first with each subsequent thought.

So many times in history, humanity was on the verge of an important discovery, but it took one brave creative thinker to make the leap. "Nothing is more obvious than the fact discovered yesterday," the physiologist Xavier Bichat aptly remarked; "and nothing is more difficult than the fact which will be discovered tomorrow."

As botanists discovered long ago, nature loves hybrids. When two plants are cross-bred, a new and excellent variety can be produced. Our fruit and flower gardens are proof of this. The same is true of people—the blending of two streams of thought, or two minds, often produces a happy result. For instance, in England the Celtic Britons absorbed Roman, Saxon, and Norman

influences. (This does not justify conquests and coloni-
zation. Cultures benefit most from peaceful cross-
fertilization.)

Our schools and universities are akin to plant nurs-
eries full of developing young sprouts. Teachers should
be gardeners, tending to the health of the whole plant—
not just the fruit. Too many, focused only on filling the
mind with specialized knowledge, dry up their students
in the process.

> The planet Earth "peoples" in just the same
> way that an apple tree "apples." You cannot get
> an intelligent organism, such as a human being,
> out of an unintelligent universe. The statement
> in the New Testament, that figs do not grow on
> thistles nor grapes on thorns, applies equally to the
> world. You do not find an intelligent organism
> living in an unintelligent environment.
>
> ALAN WATTS

## ANIMAL ANALOGIES

As we've glimpsed, a botanist could describe anything
in her mental experience using analogies from her field
of study. A zoologist could do the same. Doesn't your
mind run and rest, breathe in and exhale, consume food
and release waste, as if it were a living creature? Don't

we feel the attraction of male and female qualities in the mind and benefit from their fruitful coupling?

We commonly say that our minds grasp, carry, leap, swallow, digest, run, sleep, wake, and hear—animal analogies, all. Augustine of Hippo called the memory "the belly of the mind," in which sweet and bitter experiences are stored but no longer tasted. As odd as it seems to liken the memory to a stomach, the analogy fits.

> I think I could turn and live with animals,
>     they are so placid and self-contained,
> I stand and look at them long and long. . . .
> They show their relations to me and I accept them;
>     They bring me tokens of myself,
> they evince them plainly in their possession.
>                 WALT WHITMAN

## MIXING MINDS

The interactions of chemicals in nature are analogous to the interactions of thoughts in the mind.

Chemists tell us that, "A substance in the act of combination or decomposition, when it comes into contact with another substance, enables that second substance to enter into the same state"; and, "A substance which would, by itself, not yield itself to a particular chemical attraction will do so when placed into contact with some other substance which is yielding itself to that attraction."

These truths correspond to the contagious nature of thoughts, attitudes, emotions, and morals. When our close companions feel joyful or despairing, we're likely to feel the same. When they speak of important subjects or trifles, we're likely to speak the same. When they act courageously or cowardly, we're likely to act the same.

Many young people of promising but unformed character have been degraded by the influence of their friends. In unfit company, the finest things are paralyzed. Kindness, ambition, and lofty aims are mocked; fine music, literature, and art are ignored.

Be careful of the company you keep.

> Whoever walks with the wise becomes wise,
> but the companion of fools will suffer harm.
> THE BOOK OF PROVERBS

## THE PHYSICS OF THOUGHT
The laws of physics and mechanics also have corollaries in the nonphysical realm of mind.

"Every action causes an equal and opposite reaction"; "An object at rest will stay at rest until a force acts upon it"; "The smallest weight can lift the heaviest using leverage." Each of these axioms is true in a mental, as well as physical, sense.*

The principle of momentum applies to the mind as much as it applies a to a wheel spinning or a boulder rolling down a hill. Every writer knows that when first she sits down to write, her mind is cold and the words come slow; but as she keeps writing, her mind heats up and gains speed, leaving her to say at the end, "If only I had started with the same fire I have now—how much more I would have written!"

> *The law of cause and effect is as valid in the invisible realm of thought as it is in the visible, material world.*
>
> **JAMES ALLEN**

---

* Emerson lived before the development of quantum mechanics, but he would have been delighted by its discoveries. The surprising behavior of particle-waves at the subatomic level shines new light on the mind, going far beyond the laws of classical physics.

For instance, the Heisenberg uncertainty principle entails that, "At the subatomic level, we cannot observe something without changing it" (Gary Zukov, *The Dancing Wu Li Masters: An Overview of the New Physics*, p. 125). This principle applies to our minds, too; experienced meditators will tell you that simply observing your thoughts is enough to begin changing them.

## MENTAL MATH

Finally, the abstract science of mathematics is also symbolic of mind and thought.

For instance, the relationship between knowledge, wisdom, and virtue can be pictured this way: Knowledge is a straight line; wisdom multiplies the power of knowledge into a square; and virtue multiplies the power of wisdom into a solid cube.

A woman reads about how to grow potatoes, or hears it explained by a farmer—that's knowledge.

Then, she takes hoe in hand and begins uprooting weeds and preparing the soil. After a long day's work under the hot sun, her seed potatoes are in the ground. "Now that I've practiced the art," she thinks, "I'm confident I could plant potatoes on any hill, anywhere." That's wisdom.

But much more remains to be done. Over the ensuing weeks and months, she must exercise fortitude and determination in seeing the crop through to the harvest, overcoming adversity and setbacks along the way. That's virtue.

Knowledge squared is wisdom, and wisdom squared is virtue.

*Pure mathematics is, in its way,*
*the poetry of logical ideas. One seeks the most*
*general ideas of operation which will bring*
*together in simple, logical and unified form the*
*largest possible circle of formal relationships.*
*In this effort toward logical beauty spiritual*
*formulas are discovered necessary for the*
*deeper penetration into the laws of nature.*

**ALBERT EINSTEIN**
Nobel Prize-winning physicist

## Souls & Atoms

We've now looked at a variety of facts and principles from biology, chemistry, physics, and mathematics, and seen how they illustrate mental phenomena. What can explain this wonderful correlation between nature and mind?

The ancient Greeks proposed two competing theories which offer possible explanations:

In Plato's view, the immortal soul "forgets" all it knows when it incarnates into a finite, physical form, and our earthly education is a process of "remembering." Our souls have many incarnations; so when a person with an old soul encounters a new truth for the first time, his soul knowingly shakes its head, smiles, and says, "Hello, good fellow—I knew your great grandfather."

The other theory, that of Leucippus and Lucretius, is that everything is made of tiny, indestructible particles called "atoms." A person, a rock, a drop of water—all are composed of atoms in different quantities and combinations. Upon death and decay, each thing dissolves back into atoms, which are then recycled into new forms. Since everything is built from the same "stuff"—atoms, which are used over and over again—it's no wonder that humans share a kinship with all of nature.*

---

* In Europe, for many centuries Plato's immortal soul theory prevailed—particularly the variation adopted by Christianity. But during the Renaissance, a lost manuscript of Lucretius was discovered and his atomic theory became one of the foundations of modern science.

In Emerson's time, Michael Faraday, the great pioneer of electromagnetism, first theorized that atoms are not solid balls but spheres of energy. Emerson was excited by this idea that matter is comprised of energy, and attended Faraday's lectures in person during one of his trips to England.

Physicists have since confirmed that atoms are not physical objects; and, in fact, at the subatomic level the concept of material reality disappears entirely. See *The Dancing Wu Li Masters: An Overview of the New Physics* by Gary Zukov (1979).

Despite their differences, both theories agree that we humans have identities that extend far beyond our present physical bodies. Somewhere, sometime, we have played this game of life before, and have some vague memory of it buried within ourselves.

*Our birth is but a sleep and a forgetting:*
*The Soul that rises with us, our life's Star,*
*Hath had elsewhere its setting,*
*And cometh from afar:*
*Not in entire forgetfulness,*
*And not in utter nakedness,*
*But trailing clouds of glory do we come*
*From God, who is our home.*

WILLIAM WORDSWORTH
English poet

## FAMILY TIES

When we visit a museum with exhibits of animal skeletons and fossils, or walk through a botanical garden with specimens from throughout the plant kingdom, we're surprised by the deep resonances we feel. It's as if we're looking at our own bodies reflected in funhouse mirrors.

It's similar to the feeling of hunters and fishers when they "get inside the mind" of their prey. This points to the truth of evolution: the hunter once *was* an animal;

the fisher once *was* a fish; the biologist once *was* a microorganism; the chemist once *was* an elementary compound. As were we all, at different points along our evolutionary journey to assuming human form.

As we cannot visit a zoo without feeling our family ties, neither can a soul look up at the stars and not sense the echoes of our cosmic origins. Humans are hybrids—mixtures of salts and acids, birds and beasts, astronomic galaxies and geometric patterns. No wonder that the laws governing all these things are also within us.

Nature is saturated with divinity; each particle carries the power of the universe.

*We grow out of this world in exactly the same way that the apples grow on the apple tree. If evolution means anything, it means that. But you see, we curiously twist it. We say, "Well, first of all in the beginning there was nothing but gas and rock. And then intelligence happened to arise in it like a sort of fungus or slime on the top of the whole thing." And we are thinking in a way that disconnects the intelligence from the rocks. But where there are rocks, watch out! Because the rocks are going eventually to come alive and they are going to have people crawling over them. It is only a matter of time, just in the same way as the acorn is*

*eventually going to turn into the oak because it has*
*that potentiality within it. Rocks are not dead.*
**ALAN WATTS**

## CREATIVITY & IMAGINATION

As children of the universe, we are all born creators. We simply need to add knowledge and passion to our natural aptitude.

Look at a statue of Michelangelo's or a painting of Raphael's and feel how near you are to the same creative force. By learning your craft and tapping into that power, you too can bring forth a rush of figures from stone and paint. (Your talents and interests may lie outside the arts, but the same principle holds true. All you need is knowledge and passion added to what you already possess.)

When we use our imagination, we share in the ethereal currents of the universe. Our identity reaches further than we know—it has no limits. The greatest achievements of human ingenuity are only an extension of the same power that built our bodies.

*All things flow from one source. Everything that*
*exists has its place in the cosmos—including you.*
*That which serves the whole is good.*
**MARCUS AURELIUS**

## EVERYTHING IS MENTAL

A good image—a metaphor, analogy, or illustration—is better than any argument. A powerful symbol can persuade millions. What are all the world's religions but collections of symbols?

All of nature is a metaphor of mind. Thought is a finer chemistry, a finer growth of vegetation, a finer form of animal life.

The world is fundamentally mental. It exists to make the invisible visible, and the intangible tangible. We see plants, animals, and rocks; what we don't see—can't see, physically—is that which makes them what they are.

The universal mind hides behind all of its creations. And so, being conscious participants in that same mind, everywhere we look we see ourselves.

*Having a reasoning mind does not separate you from the universe. Your ability to sense, perceive, and understand is itself a power of the universe. You are a part of the universe, perceiving itself.*
MARCUS AURELIUS

# KEY IDEAS

1. Wherever we look in nature, our own reflection comes staring back at us.

2. The mind can't be directly observed—only described by analogy.

3. What happens in our fields and gardens happens within us, too.

4. Thoughts, attitudes, emotions, and morals are contagious.

5. Knowledge squared is wisdom, and wisdom squared is virtue.

6. Somewhere, sometime, we have played this game of life before.

7. Nature is saturated with divinity; each particle carries the power of the universe.

8. As children of the universe, we are all born creators.

9. All of nature is a metaphor of mind.

10. The world is fundamentally mental.

# Inspiration: Tapping into the One Mind

# 4

*The mind can proceed only so far upon*
*what it knows and can prove. There comes a*
*point where the mind takes a higher plane of*
*knowledge, but can never prove how it got there.*
*All great discoveries have involved such a leap.*

ALBERT EINSTEIN

W HEN James Watt met King George III, he noted that his work as an engineer was similar to a king's—both sought to increase power. Indeed, advances such as Watt's steam engine have multiplied humanity's physical power exponentially. But where is the inventor who can multiply our mental power?*

---

* It could be argued that Emerson's call has been answered: computers multiply mental power just as engines and machines multiply physical power. While this is true in some ways, computers are no substitute for thinking—and they can't generate inspiration.

We would gladly pay money for greater perception, focus, memory, and clarity of thought. Where can inspiration be bought? Alas, we can't find the shop.

In spring, when the sugar maples first flow with sap, you can't fetch buckets fast enough to catch it all. But after a few days, the flow slows to a trickle. So it is with our minds. At times of high mental energy, new ideas seem to pour out of us. But most of the time, it's a slow grind.

*The secret of it all is, to write in the gush, the throb, the flood of the moment. You want to catch its first spirit. By writing at the instant, the very heartbeat of life is caught.*
**WALT WHITMAN**

## THE POWER OF INSPIRATION

When a poet walks in nature, everything she sees corresponds to something in her mind. In composing verses about the natural landscape, she is really illuminating the mental landscape.

An inventor conceives of an idea, then builds it. When the final product goes to market it may seem new, but it's really a manifestation of what already existed in his mind.

Even if we're not poets or inventors, we've all experienced those happy moments when a new insight strikes us, a hunch crystalizes into a conclusion, or our work catches a favorable wind and toil turns into joy.

These are all examples of inspiration.

Nothing great and lasting can ever be done without inspiration. Inspiration is the *fuel* of constructive thought and action. Your engine may be strong, but without fuel it's of no use.

Logical thinking and methodical action are not enough. They plod along step-by-step, while inspiration advances in leaps and bounds.*

---

* Contrary to the stereotype of scientists relying entirely on experimental data and empirical reasoning, inspiration and intuition have played major—and overlooked—roles in the history of science.

René Descartes, who laid the foundations of the scientific method, was himself inspired by a vision in which an angelic being announced, "The conquest of nature is to be achieved through measure and number."

When Frederick Kekule was working to find the molecular structure of benzine, the answer came to him in a daydream of a snake coiled in a circle. His research confirmed that benzine was ring of atoms, and this discovery was highly influential in the development of organic chemistry.

Albert Einstein was largely self-taught in physics, and credited intuition for his revolutionary theories.

(*continued on next page*)

*Discovery requires first and foremost intuition.*
*Confirmation is another matter.*
*Logic comes after intuition.*
EUGENE WIGNER

## CATCHING INSPIRATION

Inspiration is priceless. A rush of good thoughts is better than a windfall of money. Fine clothing and furnishings can't cover up true poverty, which is poverty of mind and spirit.

What's more miraculous than inspiration? Once you've experienced the arrival of an insight, tales of magic and miracles don't seem so incredible. Inspiration comes at intervals, like lightening—first a flash, then a long darkness, and then another flash. If only we could harness its energy and produce a steady light!

Over the source of inspiration, we have no control. But is it it possible to become more receptive to it? Is there any tonic for the torpid mind?

Yes. Thinkers through the ages have found that certain states of mind are particularly conducive to

---

*(continued from previous page)* "The intellect has little to do on the road to discovery," he said. "There comes a leap in consciousness—call it intuition or what you will—the solution comes to you and you don't know how or why."

inspiration, and there are ways to increase the likeli-
hood of reaching those states.

> *Creativity is usually considered to be a process of*
> *discovering, making, or inventing something that*
> *did not exist before. But when time's divisions*
> *are overcome, there is no 'before'; everything*
> *that can be known in some sense already exists*
> *and needs only to be realized.*
>
> LARRY DOSSEY

## 1. Enjoy a Healthy Lifestyle

Health is the first muse. Physical exercise—especially
outdoors—exerts a magical influence on the mind. Plato
noted how exercise clears the mind of negative thoughts,
and a renowned lecturer once remarked, "You'll never
break down in a speech on a day when you've walked
twelve miles."

Sleep is also essential to health. You may be worn
out by your day's work, but after a good night's sleep,
you'll awaken with renewed vigor, ready for adventure.
Moreover, sometimes divine messages arrive through
our dreams.

Stress, worry, hunger, and exhaustion are impedi-
ments to insight and expression. When body and mind
are in harmony, the table is set for inspiration. As an

Arabian proverb says, "When the belly is full, it says to the head, 'Sing!'"

## 2. WRITE LETTERS

If you feel like you've run out of new thoughts, try writing a letter to an old friend. Your mind will rise to the occasion and expression will flow without effort.

You can write to a different friend each day and never run out of things to say. In this respect, the mind is like a mirror which never tires of reflecting objects—though you carry it around the whole world, it still works as good as new.

## 3. ENGAGE IN QUALITY CONVERSATION

Fine conversation is as intoxicating as wine. It's the best school of philosophy—the place where you learn what your thoughts are, how they hold up, and what power they have.

Don't approach conversation as a competition, by trying to score points and win an argument, but with curiosity. What will you draw out of the other? And what will they draw out of you? Sometimes, your own words can surprise you.

Some insights are granted to a single soul; others require two to be found. Gathered together around the fire of sympathy, our minds are warmed and quickened. Intellectual activity is contagious.

### 4. SEEK SOLITUDE

As much as we need activity and companionship, we also need time to rest and reflect.

When you go deep into the secrets of your own mind, you explore the secrets of all minds. A poet alone in the woods records her intimate thoughts; later, people in crowded cities read and resonate with her words. That which is most private and personal is most universally true.

### 5. KEEP MORNINGS SACRED

The fine influences of the morning few can explain, but all have experienced. Defend your morning from the demands and concerns of the day. While dew is on the grass, don't busy your mind with thoughts of tasks to be done.

From the time of Pythagoras on, great thinkers have insisted upon an hour of quiet contemplation every morning, to meet their own mind and learn what oracle it has to impart.

A calm mind will find a new thought waiting for it each day—or a new arrangement of old thoughts, which is just as valuable.

## 6. Spend Time in Nature

Outdoors, we're capable of sublime thoughts and sweet words that are never uttered in libraries. Ah, the spring days, the summer dawns, the fall woods! Each season holds its delicious secrets.

The best instrument of all is the Aeolian harp. No musician can rival the sounds of the wind. The voice of nature is the voice of spirit. It expresses all of life's triumph and melancholy, and lifts us into sacred space beyond any church organ.

And just as nature's sounds delight our ears, her sights delight our eyes. Have you ever stood by a lake and watched its sparkling ripples? So sudden, so slight, so spiritual—they're as wondrous as the Aurora Borealis at night.

## 7. Take a Retreat

Sometimes, when you're stuck on a particular problem or project, what's needed is a change of scenery. Book a stay in a cabin or hotel where you can work without interruption or distraction.

Certain locations—near mountains, seasides, riverbanks, and forests where there are trails to walk— are rightly known for being friendly to the muses. But your destination isn't as important as the movement itself. Often, the transition away from your familiar routine is all that's needed to spark creativity.

## 8. Read New Books

Read new books—including old books that are new to you. The best literature is thought provoking, life-affirming, and prophetical. Reading fine words cleanses and awakens our minds.

A wise proverb or a beautiful poem lifts us out of our everyday surroundings and imparts lasting insight. It puts us in tune with both our senses and spirit. Plato and Plotinus, Chaucer and Shakespeare, Hafiz and Rumi, Hindu and Celtic mythology—these and others like them are food for the soul.

Avoid the ephemeral—sensational news, tawdry novels, and mawkish poetry. It's far better to read encyclopedias and scientific books instead. Plain facts, if accurately and well presented, nourish the imagination more than many stories and rhymes. Each piece of new knowledge is kindling for inspiration.

If a book sparks thought and puts you in the mood to create, it's a good book. The best book is the one that leaves you feeling most inspired.

## 9. PERSEVERE

Willpower is not the enemy of inspiration, but an ally. In an emergency, it may be all you have to keep going. Recalling a time when he was ill and close to death, Seneca wrote, "I thought of my father, who couldn't sustain such a blow, and I *commanded* myself to live."

Goethe said, "Writing comes easily when my mind is 'hot.' When I feel the temperature running low, I counteract it with greater exertion, and the attempt is successful."

When inspiration seems absent, keep working. Put brick upon brick. Persevere.

Remember this ancient proverb: "To the persevering mortal, the blessed immortals are swift."

*The wind of God's grace is always blowing,*
*but you must raise your sail.*

**VIVEKANANDA**

Hindu philosopher

## KEY IDEAS

1. Nothing great and lasting can ever be done without inspiration.

2. Inspiration is the fuel of constructive thought and action.

3. Physical exercise exerts a magical influence on the mind.

4. Intellectual activity is contagious.

5. That which is most private and personal is most universally true.

6. A calm mind will find a new thought waiting for it each day.

7. The voice of nature is the voice of spirit.

8. Each piece of new knowledge is kindling for inspiration.

9. The best book is the one that leaves you feeling most inspired.

10. Put brick upon brick. Persevere.

# CHAPTER 5

# Wealth, Work & Success

# 5

*As we are, so we do;*
*as we do, so it is done to us;*
*we are the builders of our fortunes.*

RALPH WALDO EMERSON

WHENEVER strangers meet, one of the first questions asked is, "What do you do for a living?" It's an important question because a person isn't whole, it seems, unless they work and contribute to society in some way.

Economically, we're all consumers; we ought to be producers, too. It's good to pay your bills, but even better to add something to the commonwealth. If the expression of your genius adds value to the world, it's right to ask for fair payment in return.

Wealth comes from the application of mind to nature. Thought has always been an essential aspect of work, beginning with the creation of the first tools. A better design or a smarter system is worth hours of physical labor.

The mind seeks the most efficient way to bring resources from where they are abundant to where they are scarce—this is the basis of any economy. When a farmer picks her apples and carries them to market, they're worth far more than they were hanging in the orchard.

Industrialists become rich by organizing thousands of people and drawing on their labor. But true wealth is more than money. Just think of the riches available to each of us today: in our minds, we can draw on the labor of countless people in every part of the world, both living and dead, working in every domain— music, art, science, culture. The fruits of their labor are ours to enjoy.

As an heir to the mind, you were born to be rich; and you grow richer by the *use* of your mind.

> *He that hath a trade hath an estate; and he that hath a calling hath an office of profit and honor.*
> **BENJAMIN FRANKLIN**
> American founding father and inventor

## WEALTH & WORK

Wealth is not only mental, but moral.

Money has no value in itself—it is *representative* of value. The farmer holds tight to her money because she knows how much sweat, soil, sunshine and rain it represents. The farmer's dollar is heavy, while the Wall Street speculator's is light and leaps out of his pocket.

The value of money increases with culture and virtue. In Paris, money can buy you beauty and magnificence. In Siberia, it can only mitigate suffering. A dollar is worth far more in a place where the people are educated, industrious, and virtuous, than in a den of despair, corruption, and crime.

Financial freedom —living within your means and avoiding debt—is a virtue. If you wish the power and privilege of free thought, of choosing your work and living on your own terms, you must keep your expenditures lower than your income.

Whether you make shoes, paintings, or laws, take pride in a job well done. A financially independent person can afford not to compromise. Good work is its own reward, and quality speaks for itself.

As long as you spend from the fruits of your genius, your freedom is secure. It's possible to squander not just money but time, by spending years working outside your sphere of genius. You'll go bankrupt, literally or figuratively, if you forgo your proper career to earn a paycheck.

If it's in line with your calling and direction in life, no job is beneath you. If it pulls you away from your calling, no job is great or desirable.

What's the use in trying to be someone else? When you enjoy your work, it's more powerful. Strength lies in following your own talents and inclinations, and happiness in the same.

> *When my patron, in whom I'd placed all my best hopes, died, I began to understand that to confide in one's self, and become something of worth and value, is the best and safest course.*
>
> **MICHELANGELO**
> Italian Renaissance artist

> *I saw long ago that if I was to do anything at all I must disregard the howling throng—must go my own road, flinging back no bitter retort, but declaring myself unalterably whatever happened.*
>
> **WALT WHITMAN**

## The Way to Success

The vast majority of successful people have one trait in common—they follow the law of cause and effect. They know that an unbroken chain connects the smallest efforts to the largest results. They hold to the proverbs, "As you reap, you shall sow"; "You get what you give"; and "Nothing comes from nothing." They don't wait for luck, but make their own fortune.

Success is paired with *positivity*—a magnetic force that attracts energy, resources, and other people. The world always makes room for a positive, passionate leader.

Power is magnified by concentration. When Newton was asked how he was able to achieve his discoveries, he replied, "By always focusing my mind." Stay within your sphere of genius and concentrate your efforts on one thing at a time. Narrowness of focus is rewarded by expansion of power; for in mastering one thing, you learn principles that apply to everything.

Each day's work builds upon the previous. Keep working through times good and bad, through windfalls and calamities, booms and busts. The only way to redeem hard times is to persist through them. Try, try, and try again.

Take delight in working, not in *having worked*, and your "workbench" will follow you wherever you go. Whether standing, sleeping, or eating, the mind continues to chip away at your current project. You never know when a breakthrough will arrive, but if you're passionate about your work, you *will* achieve results.

Instead of ruminating on problems, search for solutions. What's positive? What's promising? What's progressing? Don't waste your energy complaining about the bad—instead, sing the beauty of the good. And remember, the best thing of all is love.

Blow the embers of hope into a useful flame, and redeem defeat through new thoughts and firm action. It's not easy, but it is the path to greatness.

*Now, as I look back upon the past, I can see
that, in a sense, my misfortunes have been
my fortunes—that it must have been altogether
right for me to travel a rough, hard road—
so to be tested, and at last secured!*
**WALT WHITMAN**

*Whatever is true, whatever is noble, whatever
is right, whatever is pure, whatever is lovely,
whatever is admirable—if anything is excellent
or praiseworthy—think about such things.*
**PAUL THE APOSTLE**

# KEY IDEAS

1.  Wealth comes from the application of mind to nature.

2.  You were born to be rich, and you grow richer by the use of your mind.

3.  Wealth is mental and moral.

4.  Financial freedom—living within your means and avoiding debt—is a virtue.

5.  As long as you spend from the fruits of your genius, your freedom is secure.

6.  Good work is its own reward, and quality speaks for itself.

7.  Successful people follow the law of cause and effect.

8.  The world always makes room for a positive, passionate leader.

9.  Power is magnified by concentration.

10. Don't complain about the bad—instead, sing the beauty of the good.

# Emerson's Life & Influence

RALPH WALDO EMERSON was born on May 25, 1803, the second son of a beloved and respected Christian minister in Boston. His father died of stomach cancer when Waldo was only seven, leaving the five Emerson brothers to be raised by their mother and aunt.

At age fourteen, Emerson left home for Harvard College, graduating four years later in 1821. After working as a tutor for three years, he enrolled at Harvard Divinity School with the goal of becoming a pastor like his father and grandfather.

In 1829, at age twenty-five, Emerson was ordained a minister at Boston's Second Church. That same year, he married Ellen Tucker. Just eighteen months later, Ellen died of tuberculosis. Around the same time, Emerson lost his faith in traditional Christianity. Unable to repeat the creeds and rituals of the past, he resigned his pastorate to pursue a firsthand relationship with God.

After losing his wife and leaving the ministry, Emerson sailed to Europe for ten months. He returned with a new sense of vocation: he would be a writer and lecturer, teaching reliance on the light within.

Today we remember Emerson mainly for his essays, but during his lifetime he was renowned as a public speaker. From 1833 to 1877, he delivered over 1,500 lectures. He travelled all over New England and the Midwest, even venturing once to California. He refused to lecture in the Southern slave-owning states.

A supporter of civil rights and women's rights, Emerson was a friend of many abolitionists and early feminists, including Margaret Fuller, whom he hired to edit his Transcendentalist journal, *The Dial.* Emerson signed the "Declaration of Sentiments" of the first Women's Rights Convention held at Seneca Falls in 1848, and he spoke at the 1855 convention in Boston.

While lecturing at the Smithsonian Institution in 1862, Emerson met with President Abraham Lincoln and encouraged him to push for an immediate end to slavery. The Emancipation Proclamation was issued the next year.

Among those directly inspired by Emerson were the two greatest American poets of the nineteenth century, Walt Whitman and Emily Dickinson. At age twenty-three, Whitman attended Emerson's 1842 lecture on "The Poet" in New York City. Whitman's *Leaves of Grass* (first edition, 1855) was written in answer to Emerson's call for a new, distinctly American poetry. "I was simmering, simmering, simmering," Whitman said; "Emerson brought me to a boil."

Emily Dickinson was given a copy of Emerson's *Poems* in 1850, when she was twenty. In a letter, she wrote, "Ralph Waldo Emerson has touched the secret spring." While lecturing at Amherst in 1857, Emerson stayed in the home of Dickinson's brother and sister-in-law; Emily lived next door, so the two may have met, though there is no record of it.

Emerson also influenced the founding figures of the nature conservation movement, Henry David Thoreau and John Muir. Thoreau first met Emerson at Harvard in 1837, and the two became close companions. In 1845, Thoreau moved to a small cabin on Emerson's property at Walden Pond, which led to the writing of his masterpiece, *Walden*.

John Muir—the wilderness advocate and founder of the Sierra Club—read Emerson's works and was inspired by them. During Emerson's California sojourn of 1871, the two spent several days together in Yosemite. "Emerson was the most serene, majestic, sequoia-like soul I ever met," Muir recalled. "His smile was as sweet and calm as morning light on mountains. I felt here was a man I had been seeking."

Emerson's influence was also felt in the field of psychology through the work of his godson, William James, author of *The Varieties of Religious Experience*, *Pragmatism*, and many other works. "The matchless eloquence with which Emerson proclaimed the sovereignty of the living individual electrified and emancipated his generation," James said of Emerson. "Posterity will reckon him a prophet. . . . His words are certain to be quoted more and more as time goes on, and to take their place among the Scriptures of humanity."

Emerson died in 1882, at the age of seventy-eight. On his grave marker is a passage from one of his poems:

*The passive master lent his hand*
*To the vast soul that o'er him planned.*

Ralph Waldo Emerson's voice reached far and wide, and continues to reverberate to this day.

# Sources

The body of this book is composed of passages paraphrased from the following works of Emerson's:

## ESSAYS

"History" and "Intellect" (1841) from *Essays: First Series*, Volume II of *The Complete Works of Ralph Waldo Emerson*, Wm. H. Wise, 1923.

"Inspiration" (1875) from *Letters and Social Aims*, Volume VIII of *The Complete Works of Ralph Waldo Emerson*, Wm. H. Wise, 1923.

"Power" and "Wealth" (1860) from *The Conduct of Life*, Volume VI of *The Complete Works of Ralph Waldo Emerson*, Wm. H. Wise, 1923.

"Success" (1870) from *Society and Solitude*, Volume VII of *The Complete Works of Ralph Waldo Emerson*, Wm. H. Wise, 1923.

## LECTURES

"The Uses of Natural History" (1833) from *The Early Lectures of Ralph Waldo Emerson*, Volume I, Harvard University Press, 1972.

"The American Scholar" (1837) from *Nature, Lectures and Addresses*, Volume I of *The Complete Works of Ralph Waldo Emerson*, Wm. H. Wise, 1923.

"The Powers and Laws of Thought," "The Relation of Intellect to Natural Science," and "The Tendencies and Duties of Men of Thought" (1848) from *The Later Lectures of Ralph Waldo Emerson*, Volume 1, edited by Ronald A. Bosco and Joel Myerson, University of Georgia Press, 2001.

"Memory" and "Will" (1873) from *Natural History of the Intellect: The First Publication of Emerson's Last Lectures*, edited by Maurice York and Rick Spalding, Wrightwood Press, 2008.

## QUOTES

### Epigraph

"That river flowing"—adapted from Emerson's epigraph to "Inspiration."

### Foreword

All biographical information is from *Emerson: The Mind on Fire* by Robert D. Richardson (University of California Press, 1995) and *Natural History of the Intellect: The First Publication of Emerson's Last Lectures* edited by Maurice York and Rick Spalding (Wrightwood Press, 2008).

"The mind is the supreme fact"—adapted from Emerson's epigraph to *Natural History of the Intellect*.

"A science of positive subjective experience"—Martin Seligman and Mihaly Csikszentmihalyi, "Positive Psychology: An Introduction," *American Psychologist*, January 2000, p.5.

"'You,' your joys and your sorrows"—Francis Crick, *The Astonishing Hypothesis: The Scientific Search for the Soul* (Touchstone, 1994), p. 3.

## 1. The Universal Mind
*This chapter is a paraphrase of "Intellect," with additional passages from "History" and "Will."*

"The multiplicity of minds"—adapted from Erwin Schrödinger, *What Is Life? With Mind and Matter and Autobiographical Sketches* (Cambridge University Press, 1992), p. 129.

"Deep down, the consciousness"—David Bohm, *The Essential David Bohm*, edited by Lee Nicol (Routledge, 2002), p. 149.

"A felt unity with all other minds"—Larry Dossey, *One Mind: How Our Individual Mind Is Part of a Greater Consciousness and Why It Matters* (Hay House, 2014), p. xxviii.

"What is mind?"—adapted from Bernardo Kastrup, *Why Materialism Is Baloney*, p. 53.

"Our minds can embrace possibilities"—Rupert Sheldrake, *Science Set Free: 10 Paths to New Discovery* (Deepak Chopra Books, 2012), p. 228.

"All sorrows can be borne"—Karen Blixen (pen name Isak Dinesen), quote found online.

"There is nothing either good or bad"—William Shakespeare, *Hamlet*, Act II, Scene II.

"I have thrown my life into the work"—Walt Whitman, *Whitman Speaks: His Final Thoughts on Life, Writing, Spirituality, and the Promise of America* (Library of America, 2019), p. 189.

"Your purpose is to become conscious"—Tim Freke, *Soul Story: Evolution and The Purpose of Life* (Watkins Publishing, 2017), Chapter 10.

"Until you realize"—adapted from Elbert Hubbard, *Selected Writings of Elbert Hubbard* (The Roycrofters, 1922) p. 338.

"What you think of yourself"—Henry David Thoreau, *Walden* (American Renaissance, 2009) p. 3.

## 2. PRINCIPLES & POWERS OF THOUGHT

*This chapter is a paraphrase of "The Powers and Laws of Thought," with additional passages from "Intellect and Natural Science" and "Memory."*

"The mind is its own place"—John Milton, *Paradise Lost*, Book I (1667).

"The substrate of mind"—adapted from Bernardo Kastrup, *Why Materialism Is Baloney*, p. 67.

"There is one universe"—Marcus Aurelius, *The Meditations*, paraphrased by Sam Torode (Ancient Renewal, 2017), p. 60.

"Nothing delights the mind"—Marcus Aurelius, *The Meditations*, p. 56.

"Mind is the master power"—James Allen, *As a Man Thinketh: 21st Century Edition*, paraphrased by Sam Torode (Sam Torode Book Arts, 2017), p. 3.

"Knowledge and love"—Giordano Bruno, quoted in Bernardo Kastrup's *Why Materialism Is Baloney*, p. 216.

"Diamonds are obtained"—James Allen, *As a Man Thinketh: 21st Century Edition*, p. 7.

"People long to escape"—Marcus Aurelius, *The Meditations*, p. 27.

"How does memory work?"—Rupert Sheldrake, *Science Set Free*, pp. 187–88.

"The vision that you hold in your mind"—James Allen, *As a Man Thinketh: 21st Century Edition*, p. 32.

"When your eyes become attuned"—Marcus Aurelius, *The Meditations*, p. 20.

"The eye is the lamp of the body"— Matthew 6:22, *The Bible*, New International Version.

## 3. NATURE: THE MIND'S MIRROR
*This chapter is a paraphrase of "The Relation of Intellect to Natural Science," with an additional passage from "The Uses of Natural History."*

"To see a World in a Grain of Sand"—William Blake, "Auguries of Innocence" (1803).

"What you are in your inmost being"—adapted from Alan Watts, "Myth of Myself," lecture transcription available online.

"Resolve to know the laws of nature"—Epictetus, *The Manual*, paraphrased by Sam Torode (Ancient Renewal, 2017), p. 37.

"The planet Earth peoples'"—adapted from Alan Watts, "Myth of Myself."

"I think I could turn and live with animals"—Walt Whitman, *Song of Myself: The First and Final Editions of the Great American Poem* (American Renaissance, 2010), p. 97.

"Whoever walks with the wise"—Proverbs 13:20, *The Bible*.

"The law of cause and effect"—James Allen, *As a Man Thinketh: 21st Century Edition*, p. 6.

"Pure mathematics"—Albert Einstein, "The Late Emmy Noether: Professor Einstein Writes in Appreciation of a Fellow-Mathematician," Letters to the Editor, *New York Times* (May 4, 1935), p. 12.

"Our birth is but a sleep"—William Wordsworth, "Ode: Intimations of Immortality from Recollections of Early Childhood" (1804).

"We grow out of this world"—Alan Watts, "Myth of Myself."

"All things flow from one source"—Marcus Aurelius, *The Meditations*, p. 12.

"Having a reasoning mind"—Marcus Aurelius, *The Meditations*, p. 34.

### 4. Inspiration: Tapping Into the One Mind

*This chapter is a paraphrase of "Inspiration," with an additional passage from "The American Scholar."*

"The mind can proceed only so far"—Albert Einstein, quoted in "Old Man's Advice to Youth: 'Never Lose a Holy Curiosity,'" *Life* (May 2, 1955), p. 64.

"The secret of it all"—Walt Whitman, *Whitman Speaks*, p. 189.

"Discovery requires first"—Eugene Wigner, quoted in Larry Dossey, *One Mind*, p. 193.

"Creativity is usually considered"—Larry Dossey, *One Mind*, p. 191.

"The wind of God's grace"—Vivekananda, quoted in Dossey, *One Mind*, p. 196.

### 5. Wealth, Work & Success

*This chapter consists of passages paraphrased from "Wealth," "Power," "Success," and "The Tendencies and Duties of Men of Thought."*

"As we are, so we do"—Ralph Waldo Emerson, The Conduct of Life (Riverside Press, 1860), p. 211.

"He that hath a trade"—Benjamin Franklin, *The Way to Wealth: And Other Essential Writings on Success* (Best Success Books, 2011), p. 15.

"To confide in one's self"—Michelangelo, quoted in Emerson, "Success," *Society and Solitude*, p. 291.

"I saw long ago"—Walt Whitman, *Whitman Speaks*, p. 80.

"Now, as I look back"—Walt Whitman, *Whitman Speaks*, p. 193.

"Whatever is true, whatever is noble"—Philippians 4:8, *The Bible*.

## Appendix

All biographical information is from *Emerson: The Mind on Fire* and the articles cited below.

"I was simmering and simmering"—Walt Whitman, http://www.state.nj.us/dep/parksandforests/historic/whitman/america.htm

"Ralph Waldo Emerson has touched"—Emily Dickinson, Letter to Otis Phillips Lord, April 30, 1882.

On Emily Dickinson and Emerson, see: http://edhds11.umwblogs.org/tag/ralph-waldo-emerson/

"Emerson was the most serene"—John Muir, http://vault.sierraclub.org/john_muir_exhibit/people/emerson.aspx

"The matchless eloquence"—William James, "Address to the Emerson Centenary at Concord," *Memories and Studies*, Longmans Green, 1903.

# FURTHER READING

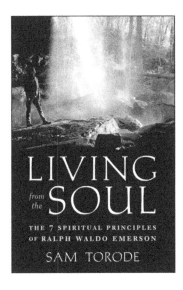

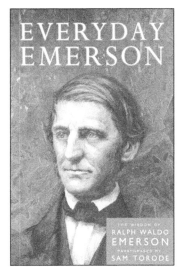

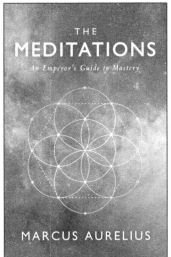

www.samtorode.com

Made in the USA
Las Vegas, NV
17 October 2023

79254881R00066